# PLANET MONSTER

**HEATHER MAISNER**

illustrated by

**ALAN ROWE**

CANDLEWICK PRESS
CAMBRIDGE, MASSACHUSETTS

For
my mum
*A. R.*

For Adam,
Lizzie, and James
*H. M.*

# Zone 1

I'm a yellow demon. Choose me!

You have arrived on Planet Monster, but Mad Mathematician is already there. He is working on a plot to destroy the universe and has set up his lab in the Underground City. Your task is to find your way through the planet's zones, reach the underground lab, and stop him from destroying the universe. Each zone is numbered and has two demons— a red one and a yellow one.

I'm a red demon. Choose me!

**Start at zone 2, choose one demon and solve his number puzzle.** The answer will tell you which zone to go to next. If you need help solving a puzzle, check the answers at the end.

Beware! Not all routes lead to the Underground City. If you are sent back to the beginning, do not give up. You are the one who must save the universe!

How many volcanoes have smoke coming out of them?

**Turn to this zone.**

You have come to a forest where Flippies live.

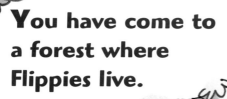

Ten baby Flippies are climbing trees. Do you see all of them?

Two spotted mommy Flippies are waiting below. Do you see them? Gather up the 10 babies and divide them equally between the mommies. How many babies will each mommy have?

**Turn to this zone.**

# Zone 4

**You are on the beach with a family of Zimzums.**

The biggest Zimzum has found 9 starfish. Do you see him? How many starfish has the smallest Zimzum found? Count them.

**Turn to this zone.**

Sea snails move in pairs.
Do you see 4 pairs?
How many sea snails
are there altogether?

**Turn to this zone.**

See the caterpillar sky train? Find 3 Zimzums on the roof of it, 3 inside it, and 2 underneath it. How many Zimzums are there altogether?

**Turn to this zone.**

## Zone 6

You are swimming in the sea with lots of Zingies.

Do you see all 20 Zingies? Ten are wearing swim caps. The rest are wearing goggles. How many Zingies are wearing goggles?

**Turn to this zone.**

Do you see all 4 octopods in the sea? Three octopods are wearing 3 flippers each. One octopod is wearing 2 flippers. How many flippers are they wearing altogether? **Turn to this zone.**

# Zone 7

**Y**ou have just arrived in a town. What odd-looking houses!

One of the triangular houses has 5 windows, one has 3 windows, and two have 2 windows. How many triangular windows are there altogether?

**Turn to this zone.**

Count all the round houses. Then count all the triangular houses. How many round and triangular houses are there altogether?

**Turn to this zone.**

You are in a haunted castle with Giggle ghosts

and Zonki ghosts.

Giggle ghosts will make you giggle forever if you touch them. How many Giggle ghosts are there?

**Turn to this zone.**

Zone
**9**

You are in a candy store with Zobbies

and
Zimzums.

The Zimzum wearing orange has 20 Monster dollars to spend. If he buys a chocolate bar for 7 Monster dollars, how many dollars will he have left?

**Turn to this zone.**

There are 2 Zobbies in the store. If one Zobbie buys a chocolate bar for 6 Monster dollars and the other buys a candied apple for 8 Monster dollars, how many dollars will they spend altogether?

**Turn to this zone.**

Look for the 7 Plinkies in the store. They each wear 2 yellow shoes and 2 green shoes. How many yellow shoes will they buy altogether?

**Turn to this zone.**

Find all 5 of the Zobbies. They each have 3 feet. How many shoes will they buy altogether?

**Turn to this zone.**

You have arrived in a city where all the clocks have stopped.

Zone **14**

**You are in a park in the rain with Plinkies and Dinozapps.**

Eight Plinkies are holding umbrellas. Count the striped umbrellas and then count the yellow umbrellas. How many more striped umbrellas are there than yellow ones?

**Turn to this zone.**

Seven Dinozapps have fallen in a puddle. Do you see them all? If 5 get out, how many will be left?

**Turn to this zone.**

**Well done!
You've reached the
Underground City.
But just barely
in time.**

Mad Mathematician has pulled the switch to destroy the universe and there are only 10 seconds left. But you can save the universe by finding the correct button. It is above a yellow button, below a green button, and between 2 orange buttons.

DESTRUCTION

# Answers

Are you stuck?

Here are the answers.

### Zone 2
Yellow demon: 3
Red demon: 4

### Zone 3
Yellow demon: 6
Red demon: 5

### Zone 4
Yellow demon: 7
Red demon: 8

### Zone 5
Yellow demon: 8
Red demon: 9

### Zone 6
Yellow demon: 10
Red demon: 11

### Zone 7
Yellow demon: 12
Red demon: 11

### Zone 8
Yellow demon: 13
Red demon: 12

### Zone 9
Yellow demon: 13
Red demon: 14

### Zone 10
Yellow demon: 14
Red demon: 15

### Zone 11
Yellow demon: 2
Red demon: 2

### Zone 12
Yellow demon: 2
Red demon: 2

### Zone 13
Yellow demon: 2
Red demon: 2

### Zone 14
Yellow demon: 2
Red demon: 2

### Zone 15

Text copyright © 1996 by Heather Maisner. Illustrations copyright © 1996 by Alan Rowe
First U.S. paperback edition 1997
The Library of Congress has cataloged the hardcover edition as follows:
Maisner, Heather.
Planet monster / by Heather Maisner ; illustrated by Alan Rowe. — 1st U.S. ed.
Summary: The reader must solve various number puzzles in order to keep Mad Mathematician from destroying the universe.
ISBN 0-7636-0057-1 (hardcover)
1. Mathematical recreations — Juvenile literature. 2. Picture puzzles — Juvenile literature.
[1. Mathematical recreations. 2. Picture puzzles.] I. Rowe, Alan, ill. II. Title.
QA95.M33 1996 793.7'4 — dc20 95-47979
ISBN 0-7636-0292-2 (paperback)
2 4 6 8 10 9 7 5 3 1
Printed in Hong Kong
This book was typeset in ITC Highlander. The pictures were done in ink.
Candlewick Press, 2067 Massachusetts Avenue, Cambridge, Massachusetts 02140